Lessons on Leadership

Leading Behind the Badge

Ronnie Ashmore

Foreword

This book is not meant to be a clinical study of leadership. You will not need three degrees and two reference manuals to understand the concepts and lessons presented herein. Instead, think of this book as a primer to get you thinking about leadership and your career path moving forward, it is a quick reference guide that can help you recognize different leadership styles when you encounter them, and maybe teach you how to find your own style. The lessons and stories presented within these pages are done so in a desire that the reader can glean a better understanding of the principles discussed.

While there seem to be a gazillion books on leadership, I believe this one is unique in that the information presented is presented in a straight-forward plain talk fashion that the reader, I hope, will find engaging.

Over the course of my career I had the opportunity to learn from many different people and see how they "did things." College instructors, police academy instructors, various training officers, whether they officially had that title or not, and supervisors all helped shape my leadership style. You will find within these pages a guide that will, hopefully, help shape your leadership style as well.

While I find recommended reading lists useless as a general rule because I never seem to follow the recommendations, I will suggest a handful of books for you to read after you finish this one as I found these books to be extremely helpful to me as I created my own path.

The Police Learning Organization: A Values-Oriented, Ten-Minute Daily Best Practice for Reducing Personal Risk and Organizational Liability by Les Kachurek, *Leadership Lessons from The Thin Blue Line* by Dean Crisp, and *Leading the Unleadable* by Alan Willet.

All three of these books will, I think, help you grow as a leader by opening up new ideas to you.

While a quick Google search on police leadership will present you with more books than you can read in your lifetime, I do hope this one is different than the others. I hope you are entertained, enlightened, and engaged. More than that I cannot ask for.

A number of people whom I encountered over the course of my life and career have helped contribute to this book and I would miss someone if I attempted to name them all, however I would like to give a special thanks to my wife and kids. They have been with me through my entire law enforcement career and have seen

firsthand all the trials,
frustrations, and successes that
this cop life has to offer. My wife
was there for all the late nights,
the early mornings, the call outs,
the missed holidays, and birthdays,
yet she has been steadfast and
always supportive of whatever beat
I wanted to walk.

Jessica, I love you forever.

Chapter One

In his book titled Find Your Why Simon Sinek encourages readers to write out their "why" for doing what it is they do. Other writers have done the same thing as well and I think this is a good place for us to begin this book. It is my intention that this book can be useful for any current or future leader, but my emphasis is on the police leader as that is where my experience lies. So, with that in mind, let me ask this, why did you choose to be a police officer? Why do you want to move up in that organization?

Leadership starts with a why. Why am I in the leader position? Why do I think I can make a difference in the followers? The title does not a leader make no matter what rank you attain, so what is your why for being or wanting to be a leader? For me, personally, I want to help others to reach their full potential in any facet of life they choose. I want to connect with people on a human level and I want to create something in a person's life to inspire them to be better than they thought they could.

Simple in words, difficult in action. I recall being told early on that leaders must connect with their followers both cognitively and emotionally to be effective. My leadership style is inclusive in some areas and autocratic in others. I always include the staff on goals and expectations I have for them. They have input on things they have more knowledge about. For instance, I let the patrol supervisors have full flexibility with the duties and the assignments.

However, I alone, as the executive leader, make administrative decisions that affect all aspects of the department as the department reflects my vision as a leader. I feel those decisions whether successful or not are mine and mine alone to make as the executive leader. I do not micro-manage, the officers were hired for a job and I fully expect them to do the job. Imparting that trust into command staff who in turn imparts it to the line officers creates a team dynamic where we all feel we are working for the same goal.

What kind of leader are you? What kind of follower are you? These may seem like strange questions, but they are at the very heart of what this book is all about, which is leadership techniques to train the younger followers to be leaders in an ever-changing career.

The term follower can also be described as worker, soldier, or employee. I prefer to think of a follower as a leader in transition. They are learning and growing as they expand their knowledge and experience, and it is your job as the leader, or boss if you prefer, to mentor these employees and create that next generation of leaders.

It has been said that people quit bad bosses not bad jobs. I think this is truer in law enforcement than other areas. While the employee may not quit the profession, they will quit doing the job with a passion that is necessary for long term success. All of us at one time or another in this profession has worked for a bad boss. A boss that only berated and never praised, one that you never knew how his mood would be that day, or a boss who could clear a patrol room of eager followers just by a look.

I heard of a department where there was a red scarf hung over the lamp in the hallway that warned officers that the boss was in a bad mood and not to be messed with. I was told of one boss who would literally turn his back to you when he was done with the conversation and walk away without a word, even while you were in mid-sentence.

What kind of leader are you? What kind of leadership have you worked for? Did it inspire you to be that kind of leader or to be different? I think it would be helpful to see various leadership styles through examples and scenarios that I gleaned while researching this book. Some are firsthand accounts, others were related to me, regardless I think it will be insightful to discuss these styles.

When I got my first job while in college it was in private security, I was a young man who could not wait to put that security badge on. I thought I was at the top of the heap, even though I was a newbie and being paid $4.25 an hour. I was a college student majoring in criminal justice and knew that the security job was a steppingstone to police work after college. In the security field you meet all kinds of people, the eager yet resigned follower like me, who had plans beyond the security job, the retired military person who was working just to get out of the house and stay busy. I learned a lot just by watching these folks that I worked with and because I enjoyed the work which was everything from standing a guard post to armored car service, I never turned down a job or took extra time off, even though I was a full-time student. Some of the things I learned at that time was how not to act and behave which was just as important in the long run as the positive lessons.

Example: I worked with a guy who was just a couple of years older than me, ex-military, who was always talking about being in law enforcement, yet never did anything to achieve this goal. He was a supervisory officer in charge of us younger followers, yet I cannot remember a single time he provided inspiration for us to do our job better, or more effectively. I do remember him griping and complaining a lot about the upper level of management. I did not care to be around that kind of personality because he was more impressed with himself and his position than we were.

Another supervisor from the security company was a gruff, older guy who was ex-military as well. Even though he had the demeanor of an agitated Chihuahua, he was always quick to explain the how and the why of his orders and suggestions. I liked his gruff personality and leadership style and looking back over the course of two plus decades in hindsight, he was the first supervisor I think I ever learned anything from.

Going from working security to working as a jailer was a transition I wasn't sure I was going to make. The rules, the regulations, it was the first time I ever worked under a strict policy and procedure guide. The supervisor in the jail did not like me, or at least it seemed like that at the time. We laugh about it now, but it was not funny then. However, starting in the jail and working my way up to street officer was a very rewarding part of my career. Then I went to the police academy. The police academy teaches a young recruit how to follow. You learn to follow guidelines, policy, criminal procedure, penal code, all kinds of stuff they cram into your young skulls. But, when you get out of the academy and you get your Field Training Officer (FTO), one of the first things said is "Forget what they taught you in the academy, I'll show you how to do this job the right way." But will they?

How many FTO's do you know of who will tell trainees that it is not their job to pass them or make them a better officer, but instead, it is their job to "cull the herd", to use an old expression. In my opinion Field Training is where the seeds of leadership should be sown, maybe not cognitively, but certainly subconsciously. FTO is where young officers are taught chain of command, taught process, taught how to talk to people who may not really want to talk at the moment. A solid FTO program can make or break a young officer. In a small agency field training is hard to do effectively, you just don't have the call volume to train a young officer as you do in larger agencies. During my second stint as chief I became aware of a problem with the FTO program where too many young officers were "passing" and then were not able to handle simple calls alone. We revamped the FTO program completely and established more stringent protocols that trainees had to meet before passing through. We also gave the training officer duties to a true leader who was eager to teach and show the followers the proper way of doing things.

I know of one FTO in an agency who is so much of a "ball breaker" that Frank Serpico himself would not make it through the initial training. He is one of the "cull the herd" type of FTOs and I believe he will be a detriment to his department in the long run.

If a leader will put aside ego and pride and properly teach the followers, agencies will have no choice but to be better for it.

Chapter Two

If you think you have to work your way up to a supervisory role to be a leader in an organization, you could not be more wrong. You can lead from where you are right now, no matter where you fall on the hierarchy chart. How does a line officer on patrol become a leader for his peers? By being an example of what your agency is all about. Conversely, if you work for an agency that just does not really seem to have any standards and each officer seems to be handling situations in their own way, it is going to be extremely difficult for a young patrol officer to have any impact on the agency as a whole, but they can still be an example of leadership values to other officers. The morose in some agencies is too systemic and tends to be contagious to where it infects the rank and file, but if you set your own standards and stick to them it can be done, just do not expect the upper management to notice.

If, however, young officers work for an organization that is committed to being an example of a group striving for excellence every day, then the young officer will feel as if they are contributing and will buy in to what the leadership wants to achieve. By having the younger officers as a partner, they become examples of success to the management and they naturally will want to show the newer hires how things are done and the standards that are expected.

As a young officer on patrol the first time I had an older non-supervisory officer tell me to forget the academy training just as we discussed earlier. Yet, the way he showed me to do the job did not fit with what I thought police work was, even though I was a rookie and had no idea what police work really meant. Granted, I only worked with him a couple of weeks right out of the academy but looking back I can't remember anything I learned from him. Had he been committed to teaching and training properly, instead of the next coffee break, the experience could have been a whole lot different. He was a line officer with experience who had a newbie who he could have molded anyway he liked to better perform the job properly, instead it was a wasted opportunity.

As a leader what are your standards, whether you are a supervisor or not? Do you take pride in showing a new hire how to do things properly? Maybe something as easy as properly packaging and labeling evidence, or more difficult tasks like working a crime scene. Little lessons that are taught in passing can have a lasting impression on a young officer. Think back on your first year or so in patrol. Did you always know what to do and how to accomplish the goal? Probably not.

But you figured it out. By listening and watching the leaders in the department solve similar problems you found your own way of accomplishing a task. Soon as you got older and more experienced you were showing the newbies how to solve problems and teaching them.

If you are reading this and thinking of your agency, I know you have known some of the people in your agency that fit what we have discussed so far. Who in your organization is a leader and who can you learn from as a young officer?

I mentioned systemic failure of an organization in the beginning of this chapter, I would now like to give an example. There was an agency that I am aware of that had a systemic problem. The officers thought evidence was just stuff and it wasn't all that important to keep up with it and they had no SOPs in place to package or store the evidence. It seemed that most officers thought their desk drawer or trunk of the patrol car was an evidence room.

The boss, I won't use the word leader for obvious reasons, had no expectations for his officers except to write tickets. All other activity, such as working cases and answering calls, was just an interruption to the traffic enforcement. As a result, the officers did not package evidence properly, or write professional reports, or do effective investigations for the citizens who were victims of crime in that city.

It all came to a head when the boss was fired and replaced by a true leader. Upon an inventory of evidence and property and an audit of case reports the new leader, in agreement with prosecutors, decided to dismiss all, not some, but all, cases the agency had filed due to evidence not being properly processed. The new leader had a difficult time changing the culture of the department and was forced to fire officers who did not buy in to the new, albeit proper, way of doing business. The boss who was fired was hired to head another agency somewhere else. I can't help but wonder what the morale and standards of the new agency are like.

The sad fact is there are enough stories like the one above to fill a library with books about ineffective leadership. How do you make certain you will not fall into that type of pit as a leader? In my opinion, you must be a lifelong learner. You must constantly be on the lookout for a better way of doing things and learning new techniques. Can you imagine working today for an organization that still used the techniques and policies of the 1980's? It would not take many shifts for you to decide to get out of there as fast as you can. What about policies and procedures from the 1990's or early 2000's? How about policies from three years ago? How would that make you feel about your agency? There is an old saying "practice beats policy every time." That means you must be constantly learning as a leader, because the followers are exposed to new ideas continuously. The policy needs to be constantly updated and the line officers need constant training on what the new expectations are.

Policies and procedures, some agencies call them general orders, must be reviewed at least annually, and updated as needed to reflect current best practices. If your agency is a larger agency it is a good bet that someone is devoted full time to policy review and keeping them up to date. What if you are a smaller agency? Who does that for your department? If possible, and if you are interested in being a policy nerd like I am, you may want to have a conversation with your chief about reviewing and updating the policies. Depending on the type of leader your organization has it could be an easy conversation or the most difficult one you will have, but it needs to be had. You would be surprised at how many departments operate under deficient policies and procedures. The personnel who work on policy have firsthand influence on shaping what kind of agency or organization it will ultimately be, and the standards expected.

What if policy and procedures are up to date and reviewed annually and all is good on that front and the chief kicks you out of his office? You can still be a leader in your organization whether supervisory or not by making sure you and the rest of the officers are following the policies and procedures. Be an example to your coworkers of a professional who follows the rules and does not cut corners. Cutting corners may make for entertaining movies and television shows of the renegade cop but it makes for a short career in the real world.

Always be learning and building so you can equip your own toolbox with what you will need when you do get to be a supervisor. Fill that toolbox with items needed to be an effective leader and discard the tools you know will not get the job done. Read constantly, any and all books, so long as they are relevant, that pertain to leadership or organizational management. Remember we as officers and as leaders are in the customer service industry. I know, I can already see some eye rolls at that analogy, but it is true more today than in the past. The citizens who entrust us to protect them from the criminal element need to be assured that the agency is operating under the best standards and practices available. We have an obligation as leaders to keep that in mind when we deal with citizens who may be in contact with us on the worst day of their lives. Remember they will judge all police officers by how you make them feel right then. A leader must be mindful of that.

Chapter Three

Let's look at various leadership styles and examples of how they lead their organizations. We need to understand that agencies are only as good as their leadership, so with that in mind here are the four types of leaders you will find in any agency. There may be more, but generally these four will cover the spectrum of styles in a police organizations day to day operations. We will paint with a broad brush here for a bit. We will expand on these styles in a few moments. I must stress again this is my opinion based on my experience. These descriptors have been around for years, but I feel they fit well in any organization.

Authoritarian: This leadership style is best summed up as the "my way or the highway" style leader. This style of leadership, sometimes called autocratic, was more popular in the post war years following WWII and fell out of favor in just the past few decades. This leader makes decisions based on little or no input from subordinates and relies on the fear of the followers to make an organization run. This leadership style is effective when decisions need to be made quickly and without delay.

Managerial: This leadership style is a rewards-based philosophy. They can keep followers motivated and promote compliance, but only for the short term, based on rewards and punishment. These leaders are not interested in long term future of an organization but instead want to keep things the way they are. These leaders tend to look at the followers work in order to find deficiencies and mistakes.

Neutral: This leadership style is a looser, hands off style of leading. It is, in my opinion, more likely to be seen in larger departments where each function of that department is more specialized. For example, the chief of a major police department is not going to be as hands on with SWAT or the investigations unit as those commanders are. This chief will delegate that authority to the commanders and exercise this style of leadership more so than a mid-sized or smaller department.

Transformational: This style of leader focuses on goals for the organization to succeed as well as goals for individual team members to be successful in their career path not just organizationally. These leaders are adept at accessing problems within an organization and transforming them into successes. This leadership style creates a vision for their organization that inspires and motivates.

Now, I know that effective leaders must be able to switch between styles when necessary. If in a crisis situation the authoritarian style may be needed, or when taking on a new task that requires an investment of time the laissez faire delegation style may be needed. We are not discussing such situations here in this book. We are simply trying to teach leadership styles for overall organizational health, the day to day approach, and trying to help you find your own style of leading.

But and there is always a but, one of these styles is not necessarily better or worse than the others. You will use all these methods and their variations depending on the situation and the goals of an organization in your career as a leader. Most new executive leaders in law enforcement who have just assumed command want to put their mark on an organization, to make it their vessel so to speak. If you are taking over from an authoritarian leader and you are more of a delegating style leader there will be problems with the followers who are not used to that style. Knowing when to use which style comes with experience and knowledge.

Notice I said knowledge not education. You can go to all the fancy universities and colleges and get all kinds of degrees and still be an ineffective leader. On the other hand, you can have a high school diploma, take an interest in your career path, read and study and learn as you gain experience and be a good, solid leader for an organization.

In my stint as chief in the organizations I have been at one of the first things I do is review the job description and eliminate the college requirements, if any are listed, for entry level officers. I had the privilege of being a part of a working group for the International Association of Chiefs of Police (IACP) hiring committee. It was a group of leaders from across the country who were assembled to work on policy for hiring new officers. I and a few others were adamant that college was not needed in order to hire an effective police officer. I was pleased to see that others held that view as well.

Likewise, I do not think it is necessary to have a college degree to be in charge of a police organization. Now, I am not saying that education is not needed or can't help a leader develop. I would not want the reader to think I do not value education, but how many leaders who do have these fancy degrees have damaged their organizations by being ineffective and incompetent?

Back to our discussion. I do not want to mislead you into believing one style will work better than the other. The fact is each department and each leader of that department and within that department will use the style that works for that department. What works for larger departments like the NYPD or the Houston Police Department will not work for the small department with fifty officers or less. Nor will those small department leadership styles work for the NYPD.

Leadership is not a popularity contest and decisions should not be based on how favorable the followers will view those decisions. Decisions are mission based for the goals of the organization as a whole and no individual should be allowed by a leader to hold the organization back from achieving those goals because of popularity.

I would like to take a moment and give an example of an authoritarian style leader who was the supervisor of my first department I ever worked in. He was a guy who the patrol guys feared to make mad and felt sick whenever called to his office. He was a "my way or the highway" type of leader who would brook no dissension or back talk from us when it came to our duties as officers. I, and some of us who tell stories of him when we get together, cannot remember but maybe a couple of times of him telling us good job, but we can remember a bunch of times he would chew us out for what we thought were little things. I remember his closed-door office meetings made me feel like I wanted to punch my mother in the face for even considering giving birth to me.

In the first few minutes of the "discussion", or as we called it behind his back the "discussin", he would make you feel so inadequate and question why you ever wanted to be a police officer in the first place. But, by the end of the event you would run through a brick wall for him and would leave his office wanting to go to work and make him proud of you. He never gave awards or performance-based gratitude, he figured that whatever good you did it was what you were supposed to do as a police officer.

He was totally authoritarian and we as followers did not dare disobey any directive given. Knowing that I had career plans beyond the patrol room I watched and mentally noted how he led us to follow through on whatever we were doing.

In today's law enforcement world, I don't believe his style would work for the younger work force this industry is seeing come in, but it definitely worked for us at that moment in time.

I promoted to sergeant and made it to detective under his leadership. It was when I made supervisor that I got a newer appreciation for his style of command. Suddenly, the things that seemed to be of little consequence that he would get so mad about I realized that he was heading off larger problems in the future.

He is still a friend and mentor to me today and I cannot express enough how much I appreciated learning from him, both the good and the bad. In sports they talk about a coaching tree of what coach spawned the careers of other coaches, well I do not know what they call that analogy in law enforcement but his tree is made up of a number, probably in the high teens, of executives and supervisory officers throughout my home state. Do you think his authoritarian style was effective on his followers? You're damn right.

Chapter Four

Congratulations! You have been hired to be the CEO of a police organization, you are now the chief and everyone is expecting good things from you. The citizens, the council, the mayor, the officers are all expecting you to lead the charge, they do not care that this is your first chief position. What now?

First, you are going to have to know what kind of department you are assuming command of. Is it well respected? Was the former chief well liked? Are the officers respected in the community? You should already know all of this through your research prior to being hired. For the purpose of this chapter, because this topic could fill a book on its own, let's assume the former chief was highly respected and retired after being in charge for many, many years. What are some challenges you as a new leader may face?

We discussed last chapter the various leadership styles. When you assume a new command or first command you need to let everyone know that you are the CEO. You lead by example and you produce organizational goals that officers and citizens can get behind and support. While you may need to be open and encourage new ideas on what direction to take the department moving forward the ultimate decision is yours for better or worse. Remember, sometimes new command means new assignments for the officers, it can be a stressful time in their lives until they get familiar with your expectations so be mindful of that. What kind of followers will you find in your new department? Let's look at some personality characteristics you may find, again this is not inclusive, and each may have a subsection as well. As in last chapter, these descriptors are not new or unique to me but have been around for a while.

Negative: These officers will never be onboard for a change in structure and what they are used to. These officers will comply with change only when forced to by an authority within the department. You may never win them over to your way of doing things, but once you know they exist you can isolate their influence on others.

Passive: These officers will just go along to get along and will cause no real problems within the organization. They will adhere to the changes but offer little input if pressed to give any. Some passive types will become the biggest supporters of change because they will lead by example and in some cases negate the negative opinions.

Committed: These officers simply want to do their job with no interruption from the administration. They are not so much worried about how you as a new chief will influence the department as a whole as they are more concerned how your policies will affect them doing their job to help citizens who need their services.

The negative officer is pretty easy to identify, this officer is the one who comes to work thirty minutes early just to gripe about coming to work. Any new policy or procedure is met with eyerolls and headshakes and maybe a verbal complaint about how things have always been done. These types of officers can affect younger officers if the negativity is not tempered.

The passive officer will look at the same policy and procedure update the negative officer scoffed at and think "Okay, this is the way we do it now" with no reservations about implementing the new practice. These officers can be a positive influence on how to deal with the ever-changing landscape of police work to younger officers.

The committed officer is like the passive type when it comes to new ideas, but the committed type is more likely to have suggestions on implementing the practice or find problems within the policy when it comes to implementing it on the street. A passive officer can become a committed officer over time and a committed officer can become a committed follower who is then a leader in transition. Committed officers will make your job as chief easier.

So, as stated earlier you are the new leader who is replacing a respected and recently retired leader. You have completed an audit of policies and procedures and identified the personality types you will be addressing. You need to assert your leadership style, whatever that is based on your training, experience, and personality, as soon as possible because cops for the most part hate change so the quicker you walk them through whatever changes are coming, the better off you are as a leader. You need to determine deficiencies in the rank and file, in the organizational goals and values, and in the supervisory leaders in the department.

All of this sounds so easy when writing it out, but it is so very difficult to put into practice. We discussed in chapter two that leadership is not a popularity contest, you now get to put that theory to practice. Some of your decisions will incur mumbling and complaining from the negatives, some decisions, especially personnel decisions, will be highly unpopular. If the change is needed it needs to be implemented but change just for change sake is not wise.

If you locate a deficiency in your department that is holding your organization back from being what you envision, then the change needs to happen sooner rather than later, and the followers and command staff need to understand why. The two things cops hate more than anything, in my experience, is the way things have always been done and changing how it has always been done.

There was a department I heard about where the chief was popular but left after many years to work in the private sector. His replacement was hired, and his first order was to call the lieutenant in for a meeting before the department wide meeting with the other officers. They visited for a little bit, made small talk, and then out of nowhere the chief demoted the lieutenant on the spot without explanation.

In the department meeting the chief made the announcement that the lieutenant position was open for anyone interested who met the requirements. A shocked group of officers were confused because the lieutenant had been in that position for a long time and was well respected, but some decided to go for the promotion opportunity even though none had any rank within the department. The former lieutenant also put in for the position as well.

The chief promoted the former lieutenant to his rank and gave the few others who applied ranks as well, corporals, sergeants, etc. When asked by the lieutenant why he did this the chief replied, "I needed to see how much you wanted your leadership role in this department."

This chief never gained the trust of his followers because of this incident. I am sure he thought it was a good idea at the time, but the department saw it as a trust issue that he could never recover from. The lieutenant is now the chief.

I relate that story to reiterate the fact that as a leader all your decisions, even ones where you are trying to boost morale, may not have the intended effect. The story above is a lesson on how it is not a good idea to play games with people's emotions and belittle their investment within the organization. It is always, in my opinion, better to deal openly with changes you may be wanting to install in a fair way.

Chapter Five

Over the course of my career I have observed and absorbed various styles of leadership methods. I also read voraciously anything I could about effective leadership not just involving law enforcement but leadership in general. I knew early on that I wanted to do more with my career than just patrol, and I was determined to be successful at it. I would suggest you do the same, never stop learning.

As a line officer I made mistakes and had my share of WTF moments. I have been verbally reprimanded and written up for some of my mistakes. I was the kind of officer that inspired chiefs to create new policy. As a supervisor I wanted to be liked and respected, I wanted the followers to trust me and I wanted to take care of "my guys." That did not work out well because soon my directives were being ignored and the officers were trying to take advantage of my good nature. I was able to notice it and turn it around in time that no harm came, and you would think I would learn my lesson, but no.

During my time as chief I made mistakes that cost me time in developing the type of agency I wanted to have. I left officers too long in roles they never should have had to start with. Some I inherited, some I hired. I found through trial and error that if an officer wasn't showing the leadership ability that I wanted for the agency then I should replace that officer immediately.

I feel I have been an effective leader in my career, though ultimately that determination is not up to me to make, instead it is determined by the men and women who have worked under my leadership, I use two measuring sticks to reach that conclusion.

First, when I was a line officer and then a supervisor, I was able to take my leaders directives and put them in place effectively and smoothly for the most part. In other words, I followed my leaders in order to lead my followers. Secondly, as a chief I have had great success in changing the cultures and environments of the agencies I led. I effected transformational change that produced results that others thought were unachievable. Some of the officers whom I have supervised still call and drop by to visit just to talk, some still want my advice on how to handle situations, both on a personal and professional level.

These are my experiences and results, what are yours? Do you have the ability to lead others to a goal or do you do better with directives given to you to follow? Make no mistake I know not everyone wants to be a supervisor or a chief. Remember, it is not about achieving rank or having a title, it is about leadership. I have known plenty of people both in law enforcement and out who have turned down promotions in order to stay where they are. Maybe as a patrol officer or detective you are where you want to be and now you are happy and don't want to be promoted. Great, organizations need committed people at all levels or else there would be no organization.

If you are in the property room, make it the best property room in the State. Make it an example of what a property room should look like. Same for dispatch and investigations and patrol. Lead from where you are how you can. You can make as much of an impact on your organization as the CEO can if you take initiative.

Some leaders get confused on what they want their organization to be. They lose initiative after a while and become stagnant. Followers want to follow, but only if they can believe in the leader and their ability to achieve the ultimate goal. Too many times organizations start out to change the way things are done only to get bogged down in the minutia of everyday activity. The goal is to never be satisfied with where you are as an organization, but to keep progress going by ever evolving.

As a leader you must build trust with the officers and community at large. The officers need to trust you to have their back in situations where they are in the right and facing backlash. The community needs to trust that if an officer is wrong that you as a chief executive will have their interests in mind. It is a fine line to walk because not everybody is going to think your decisions are correct. But, if you have integrity and are transparent about what is going on, no one can accuse you of playing favorites.

Here's something to remember. You can do everything right by policy and procedure and still be viewed as being in the wrong. In these instances, no amount of community goodwill will be of assistance to you, you as the leader must take the knocks that come and remain focused on your organizational goals. That's where self-awareness as a leader will help guide you through these times.

It is not easy being in charge of a group of people, especially a bunch of cynical cops, but it can be personally rewarding. The line officer thinks the administration does nothing during their shift, that the officers are the reason the department functions and they are right, but the organization falls apart without the leaders as well. As a line officer I believed our evening and overnight shifts worked way harder than the dayshift and administration did. My belief changed as my career evolved. When I began working on dayshift, I found myself thinking the evenings and midnight shifts did nothing, though I knew better. I believe the line officers do work hard but in a different way than I do as an executive. The officers are the reason the department functions, the reason why complaints are down, the reason why crime is down, etc. That is because of policies and procedures put in place by an administration that is constantly trying to find ways to make their departments and cities better. Take a look, a good look, at your organization and see if that is not the case where you are.

Let's look at an example where needed change came, and it caused problems in the short term. There was a department that needed an overhaul. The chief had served for over three decades, the morale was low and working conditions were poor. The department did not keep up with the changes in policing and as a result the officers were not properly trained. A new chief came in and immediately assessed the situation and started implementing changes.

Some were popular, like changing the patrol schedules to a fixed schedule instead of rotational. Making the shift times more flexible and open. Other decisions were not well received. The new chief wanted all the officers trained in new technology, like body cameras, and new investigation techniques that would require a monetary investment from the department and a time investment from the officers.

The officers, some of whom had been with the department for a long time, went through the motions and considered training days as a vacation away from work. When it came time to implement the changes, like body cameras for instance, the officers always had an excuse why they were not recording. When pressed hard on the issues of not following directives the officers were close to, for lack of a better word, mutiny. Officers would call in sick or check on duty then get lost for the entire shift and so on.

After a couple of months of not seeing any of his changes take effect the way he wanted, the chief decided to completely shake up the department. He demoted and promoted and suspended, in most cases, fired officers as he saw the need. After a year, he started to see the department of his vision take shape. Fast forward a few more years that department is still thriving under that chief's leadership.

I want to challenge you to look at your organization, not from where you are in the organization, but from a thirty-thousand-foot view, being critical and honest of the way it functions, of its policies and procedures. Is it a well-run organization or can it be improved? What would you do to improve it? Okay, so when will you start?

Chapter Six

Police work when it is all said and done is not that difficult. We are peacekeepers, lawmen who have taken an oath to protect the innocent from the predators. That is a simplified version, but I believe it is true. Unfortunately, this profession has its share of idiots in the leadership role that interfere with the simplicity of this job. Think a little about various leaders. The strong leaders, leaders who have shown that the right choices aren't the easy ones. The weak leaders, leaders who need three opinion polls and an advisor to make a decision. One thing I cannot stand is a coward and, in my opinion, cowards rise to the top of this profession more than one would realize. Whether physical cowards or moral cowards, I think the stench they give an organization will take years to eliminate. I know I am going to make some people mad with my opinions in this chapter, but here goes.

Courageous leaders are easy to define, they make the tough choices even though it may not be the popular choice. Courageous leaders are guided by a set of inner morals that are not open for compromise. Maybe you have worked for a leader who has exercised these attributes and if so, I hope you find yourself listening more to that leader than to the detractors.

So called "social justice warriors" and reformers are part of the reason this profession is in a downturn now. From all the politicians, who lack any credibility, making suggestions on how policing should work, to the cowards in leadership who follow a political agenda without any thought to the followers they purport to lead it is no wonder why recruiting is suffering. Who would want to do this job today?

Research has shown that police officers have lost interest in doing the job as it was intended to be done. Due to current negativity from certain high-profile cases, like Ferguson Missouri, and the seemingly endless bashing of cops, the state of current morale in law enforcement is alarmingly low. Street cops do not want to be as proactive as they once were, and this new generation of police officers have to deal with every encounter possibly being on social media and scrutinized by people who have no idea what dangers this job entails. A quick Google search on police morale will return multiple hits on how the current state of policing is at an all-time low.

Luckily, a chosen few still answer the call every day. They come to work knowing that with any mistake, because of a coward in the leadership position, their career could be over. The young recruit coming through the academy still has a servant mindset, they want to help their community by being an example of what a principled life is.

The "reformers" put innocent people at risk with their ideology of what leadership should look like. No real leader should buy into these misplaced ideals, instead the real leader should remember that they are, at its simplest, the barrier between function and disfunction in an organization. Reformers like to throw the phrase "broken justice system" around and at the same time try to break that system with their policies and practices. It seems at times that the reformers and SJWs are so worried about civil rights violations of the accused they lose sight of the victims and their entitlement to those same civil rights. Reform of some of the system practices are a needed thing, but the entire system should not be torn down to satisfy a political mindset.

A police leader should be careful of not violating anybody's Constitutional Rights, but at the same time protecting those same rights for the victims. It would send a more consistent message if, for example, we focused more on victims and their plight for justice rather than the criminal.

Some of the best leaders in law enforcement have been able to walk that fine line very well. Others have not. It is not for us to eliminate the entire justice system, but rather fix what parts are broken or are not functioning properly.

We all know, or should know, who Frank Serpico is. For decades his name has been held up as a flag of what a conscientious, moral, honest police officer is and rightly so. But there are also police officers who are the polar opposite of moral and honest. These should be removed from the profession swiftly and without hindsight. That is where a strong leader comes into play. I know if your agency is unionized or civil service, then you are not going to be able to release an officer as quick as you would like but it can still be done. Leaders, whether executives or first line supervisors, have to know their followers and act decisively when necessary. I, as well as those I have worked for, have been slow to act in certain situations that could have been disastrous, but I learned from the mistake and made a vow not to be so naïve again.

I think that a leader needs to ensure that all people, including the suspects and criminals, have their constitutional rights protected, that is job one. The next thing is to seek justice for the victims while ensuring those same protections for both criminal and victim. From my personal perspective though, I do not like a system that worries so much about criminals and less about victims and their families.

We have heard recently of certain prosecutors who are picking and choosing what crime to prosecute by implementing a non-prosecute policy for certain crimes like retail theft and minor drug offenses. We can have a discussion all day long about drug crimes and possible solutions and never reach a conclusion. That is not the point of this chapter. Prosecutors who implement these policies are basically telling their constituents that they, the prosecutor, get to decide who the victims are and what the system will do about it. This is a dangerous policy to follow and does nothing to improve morale or give the citizens a positive view of the justice system.

When a leader of a law enforcement organization tells the public through their actions that it is only looking out for a certain group of people instead of all the people that is just a step away from a total collapse of the entire justice system.

Likewise, when an organization is not transparent and open about mistakes or dishonest acts within that department the public feels it is being lied to and the whole organization is marked as corrupt. This too damages the system as well.

The only way a department maintains their integrity is for the leaders to admit mistakes and encourage solving the problems which led to those mistakes. That is far more difficult than one would think, but it is what separates the strong leaders from the weak. Let's phrase it this way, the courageous leader will be lauded by the followers who believe in the mission of the organization, cowardly leaders will be loathed by those same followers. A true leader is not quick to jump on the current bandwagon of training that has no real benefit to the law enforcement world.

My home state recently within the last few years mandated a training course called Civilian Interaction Training as part of the Sandra Bland Act in response to a high-profile incident involving Sandra Bland and the Texas Department of Public Safety

Highway Patrol. The incident is a perfect example of how not to treat the citizens as a police officer. The Trooper pulled Bland over for a traffic violation, fail to signal lane change. The encounter took a drastic turn as the Trooper demanded Bland put out her cigarette, and when she refused the Trooper started yelling commands to get out of the car and Bland was asking for explanations on why. The Trooper pulls his taser and threatens to "light her up", eventually Bland got out of the car due to the Taser threat and is heard saying, "Wow. Wow. You're doing all of this for a failure to signal?" she was arrested and days later found dead in her jail cell. The Trooper gave a statement that he was in fear of his life, it was later determined that he lied.

This incident sparked outrage and made headlines for months afterward and rightly so. A DPS internal investigation showed the Trooper did not follow procedure and was at fault for the incident. You can Google the video and watch the Trooper dash cam and the cellphone footage recorded by Sandra Bland.

This incident is clearly a failure on the part of the DPS Trooper and maybe the DPS leadership in general, but in no way should it have disparaged the other Troopers who conduct themselves professionally and without incident daily. It certainly should not have resulted in mandated training to essentially cover the same seven-step violator contact that every police officer learns in the academy and performs daily with no incident. The failure was that of the individual Trooper and not of the entire system. The Sandra Bland Act contains other provisions that deal with the jail side of the system as well and added numerous hours to training for counties and the jail staff.

Incidents like this and others that the politicians use to bolster their careers by passing legislation that is, in the long run, useless contributes mightily to the low morale of the current group of law enforcement professionals and only puts a Band Aid on the problems of police and citizen interactions. The training on how police should

conduct traffic stops has been a part of the basic police academy for as long as anyone can remember. The process of the initial contact on traffic stops has not changed, even with this implementation of mandated training. The answer to combating incidents like this is not found in our state capitols and politicians, instead it is found in our department leadership, provided they are competent and not hacks, internal training, and internal checks and balances in order to prevent these incidents from happening and removing people who have no place in this career. In order to have that internal watchdog
ability the organization must have credibility to be honest and forthcoming.

I feel for Sandra Bland's family and her loved ones, watching the video of the traffic stop will make you cringe and ashamed that this incident happened. Sandra Bland's only crime that day in July of 2015 was encountering a Trooper who had no business being on the job and representing the men and women of this profession.

Chapter Seven

We have talked about a variety of things in this book so now I would like to try to pull these concepts together. It is not all that important what has happened before you take the leadership reins, as all that, positive and negative is the past. The future is what matters, and it is going to be whatever you make it, positive and negative.

Think back on the scenario mentioned earlier of being named a chief executive. What is your style going to be? What are your first actions as the leader? We have discussed a few different methods and looked at examples of those methods, so what are you going to do? Only you can answer that question, hopefully by gaining insight from this book, and by watching and thinking of the leaders you have worked under. You can determine what you want to do and not do by being a human test template of other leaders.

What if you are already a leader but you're wanting to take it to the next level. If you are able to change your philosophy and style to change from one method to another then you can have organizational success. Leaders want to lead, followers want to follow so, if they desire at some point in the future, they can lead as well.

When a leader is fortunate enough to have a follower who wants to learn, the leader should do everything they can to cultivate the growth of the follower. The follower will have to make a time commitment to increasing their knowledge and skills but if the determination is there the investment will be also. I would encourage everyone who wants to be a leader in any organization to immerse yourself in learning a vast amount of leadership styles and techniques, that way you find your voice as a leader.

I remember sitting and talking to the chief executive leader of the department I worked for at the time about budgets and how to make and keep them. He always seemed to manage to be under budget every year and I wanted to know how. I soaked up all the information I could from him. I like to think I am good at staying in budget and finding ways to accomplish goals and coming in under budget every year. It is because of what I learned from listening and learning from him. Some of my officers call me a "cheapskate" because I am picky how I spend taxpayer money, but we always make it work.

Finding someone who took an interest in my goals and ambitions as a young officer without them feeling threatened about their own position was of massive importance to me. I think if you can find someone who will take time to teach and instruct you as a young officer you can benefit from it immensely. Likewise, if you can take time as a leader to cultivate and shape a young officer you will benefit from that as well.

We tend to get bogged down in the everyday and fail to see the big picture. How many times have you heard someone say something like " this place would fall apart without me?" Really? There is not a single person in any organization that is irreplaceable, no matter how important we think we are, we can all be replaced, probably faster than we would like to admit. My point is, we are all just passing through, we are placeholders for the next generation. So, we owe it to that young follower to train them properly and not act like we know the secret handshake and keep our knowledge to ourselves.

I do not want to paint a gloomy picture but, instead, I want to be realistic. I, as a leader, do not want to retire and have my young followers that have spent time in an organization I was in charge of feel they learned nothing, either from me or my command staff. I want all of them to feel they could be the CEO if they wanted that for their career.

So, how do you do this? How do you train others to be leaders when you are the leader now? Well, everyone is different, but I think you accomplish this by being the leader who is a teacher as well. The concepts we have discussed so far that were successful have one thing in common. The leader was a mentor as well as a boss. It is not about putting together a policy and procedure and expecting others to fall in line. If that were the case, then everyone could be a leader.

As a leader you know mistakes are going to happen, how you deal with those mistakes will determine if you are a boss or a leader. A boss will rant and rave and chew you out for mistakes and expect you to be okay with that. A leader corrects the behavior and teaches you not to make those types of mistakes again. One is destructive, the other is constructive. We all make mistakes, but not all mistakes should be treated like it is the end of the world.

I encourage you as a current leader or a leader in the making to inventory how you treat the ones who follow you. Is that relationship good? Could it be better?

Chapter Eight

I want to address something that you already knew was bound to be discussed. The millennials that are in the workforce and the generation following the millennials. This group has been the most studied group in the last few years, and you can Google search and find all kinds of millennial information, from the serious to others making fun of them.

You go to a gathering of executives and mention millennials their reaction usually is along the lines of "Oh, the horror!!!" Well, no, not even close. Let's look at the millennials and the other generations we will be working with in the workplace and how you, as an effective leader for an organization, could benefit.

Now when you get into labeling generations you can get lost in the jungle of trying to figure out where each group fits into what timeline. For simplicity's sake I will try to keep it as easy to understand as I can and show how each group can work with the others for a successful environment. Keep in mind these ages change slightly depending on what reference you use as there is no definitive standard on measuring generations.

Let's start with the Baby Boomer Generation. They were born between 1946 and 1964, so they would be mid 50's to mid-70's in age. They are the current leaders in most departments still, but they are retiring at a faster rate than most organizations can recruit, leaving a gap in the structure. This generation is stereotyped as being gruff and short tempered with younger people. They are typically more militaristic in their approach to law enforcement as that is how it was when they were coming up.

You hear of leaders of this group sticking to those beliefs even in a changing world, for example, they might not allow their officers to have tattoos or facial hair at all.

Generation X, which is my generation, was born between 1965 and 1979. This group is more prevalent in the upper management and command staff positions due to the retiring of boomers. Gen X was the first technology generation, we grew up with computers in the home, and are comfortable for the most part learning new technology like smartphones and other modern tools. Gen X is not as committed to a single employer as the previous generations and will leave an organization if they feel they need to for personal development. They like to work hard and will give far more than is required if they feel they are making a difference. Their work ethic tends to be strong, but they like to have fun as well.

Millennials were born between 1980 and 1994. According to Pew Research Center in an April 2018 study, they make up the largest group of workers in the country, they are between 26 and 40 years old, and are going to be the executive leaders in tomorrow's police world as they are already in command staff positions. Most older executives break out in a cold sweat when talking about this generation, because of the stereotype of them being so young and feeling entitled. But are they really? I have found that, for the most part, this is not true. For instance, this group is much, much, more technologically advanced than previous generations and they are constantly learning new technology faster and easier than previous generations. They are also more likely to flourish in a team environment where the previous generations wanted to work alone. In my experience I like having this group as part of my organization because of these traits. They are eager to learn, and easy to train if you understand how to communicate with them. They are the most prevalent factor in the workforce, so it only makes sense for us old guys to help shape them because the generation under them, generation Z, is coming up now and will present their own challenges.

So, the young millennial follower has a chance, for a moment, to learn from the boomer and Gen Xer how to perform their duties and make an impact. When I was an investigator, my partner was a baby boomer in his mid-50's, I was in my early 30's. He would always say, "I don't know about you young guys, this job is gonna go to hell because of you guys." By contrast I would ask him, " How did you old guys do this job in the dark ages without the internet?"

My point is now it is my generation grumbling about the younger generation. Every generation complains about the generations that follow them, it has always been that way, it is a cycle that will probably never change. However, I learned a lot from my old partner about how to work a case, how to competently handle a crime scene no matter how big it was, and how to teach a young investigator how to investigate.

The essence of this work has not changed much since the beginning, protect the innocent from the criminal element, but the methods of doing that job continuously changes. By the time the young millennial generation becomes the older generation, the world that we think is so advanced right now will seem antiquated, so too, will the methods of policing, but the core leadership methods of teaching and training the next group of leaders coming up will never go out of style.

So, let the millennials and the younger followers make fun of you for being old and not knowing how to turn on the computer. At the same time, make sure you and your command staff are, as leaders, teaching them how to do this job the best you can. You filled your leadership toolbox with tools you needed from the older leaders you followed, make sure you allow the younger followers to build their own toolbox. The organization will be better for it.

Chapter Nine

I will tell you something told to me years ago that I only understood as I got promoted. The further away you move from the patrol room the less funny everything becomes. What that means is that as a leader you're where the buck stops, any blame, deserved or not, will fall on you. You will be talked about behind your back, hopefully not by your followers, but probably in some capacity that will happen. You will get visits and phone calls from politicians and friends of politicians wanting you to intervene in some situation or another, and they will expect you to do it. The way I handle these situations which I learned from another executive early on is not to get involved in personal grievances. If something is a violation of law handle it like any other complaint. If they want you to go outside the purview of your duty, then simply say no.

"No" comes in very handy when dealing with situations that goes beyond what you can do. My favorite saying from a former chief I worked for was "There's what you want, and there's what we can do. How can we meet in the middle?" You will live in the middle a lot as a leader and that's okay, so long as you don't compromise organizational integrity or your morals and standards it's no big thing. Nobody ever gets everything they want life just doesn't work that way.

Too many times we as executives feel we need to please everyone, and we get bogged down in the mire that we help create when we don't set limits. Someone says they heard a rumor about you, well people, as people do, gossip, a lot. If it doesn't affect your personal or professional life, so what. You're told so and so doesn't like you, okay, and? Having a clear understanding of who you are as a person is very important in being a leader with a vision rather than a leader who gets swayed by every little nuance.

As a patrol officer it was funny to prank other patrol guys. We used to wait until an officer took their duty belt off in the office, then somebody would take all the pieces off it, all the equipment, dismantle the gun, remove the bullets from all magazines......Okay, honestly that was more funny to do it to someone than to have it done to you. As you move up in rank and responsibility you have less time to enjoy the slow times, because it seems there are less slow times to enjoy.

What do you do when the mayor comes to you and asks to fix a speeding ticket one of your officers wrote him? Well, now that's not as tricky of a question as you would think. The answer is two-fold. First, the mayor lacks any integrity if he makes this approach, second, you have to back your officers and tell him to see it through to court if he wants to fight it. Nobody at any level within an organization should be involved in such petty corruption as ticket fixing, and if they are the leader should remove them from the organization immediately.

I am not much of a ticket writer, but I wrote a parking ticket to a vehicle that was parked in a clearly marked no parking zone. I found out later that the owner of the vehicle was the new city administrator, which made him my boss. I did nothing to intervene with the court process, and to the administrator's credit, he did not contest the citation or approach me about it. Instead, he paid it and never mentioned it to me. I appreciated that level of professionalism.

Leadership at any level can be very stressful, so you need to be cognitive of the fact that was mentioned in the last chapter about passing through. Do not let the stress of any position in an organization steal your health from you. When you retire, within a few months it will be as if you never worked there. So why let this wreck your health? It is important to be as good a leader and mentor as possible because the future generations count on us. You're probably thinking "Wow, this took a weird turn". Not really.

Everything we do in our life is structured toward the future. When you have children, you teach them the way they should act and behave. You try to raise them the best you can, you don't let them run feral and figure things out for themselves. Likewise, when you are the leader of an organization, you teach the young followers how to do the job with an eye on the future, knowing you won't always be there. That's where a good, well placed "no" can be effective. When you are stressed about something and people keep wanting and wanting, to borrow a line from the 80's, "Just say no," maybe for a moment or even a day until you can make the best decision. Keep an eye on the future, maintain your health for your organization and, more importantly, your family.

I tell my wife I don't want to be the grumpy old guy when I retire (she usually tells me I am way ahead of the timeframe) but I want to be active in this profession in some capacity and stay involved with young officers and compare how they do things to how I did it at that point in my career, or maybe teach or speak to groups on the topics that are important to us in this profession.

Chapter Ten

The IACP adopted the Law
Enforcement Code of Ethics in
October 1957. The Code of Ethics
stands as an example to the
mission and commitment law
enforcement agencies make to the
public they serve. I believe every
officer should be reminded of this

code regularly. This is the code as
adopted:

*Law Enforcement Code of Ethics
As a law enforcement officer, my
fundamental duty is to serve the
community; to safeguard lives and
property; to protect the innocent
against deception, the weak
against oppression or intimidation
and the peaceful against violence
or disorder; and to respect the
constitutional rights of all to
liberty, equality, and justice.
I will keep my private life unsullied
as an example to all and will
behave in a manner that does not
bring discredit to me or to my
agency. I will maintain courageous
calm in the face of danger, scorn, or
ridicule; develop self-restraint; and
be constantly mindful of the
welfare of others. Honest in*

*thought and deed both in my
personal and official life, I will be
exemplary in obeying the law and
the regulations of my department.
Whatever I see or hear of a
confidential nature or that is
confided to me in my official
capacity will be kept ever secret
unless revelation is necessary in
the performance of my duty.
I will never act officiously or permit
personal feelings, prejudices,
political beliefs, aspirations,
animosities, or friendships to
influence my decisions. With no
compromise for crime and with
relentless prosecution of criminals,
I will enforce the law courteously
and appropriately without fear or
favor, malice, or ill will, never
employing unnecessary force or*

*violence and never accepting
gratuities.
I recognize the badge of my office
as a symbol of public faith, and I
accept it as a public trust to be held
so long as I am true to the ethics of
police service. I will never engage
in acts of corruption or bribery, nor
will I condone such acts by other
police officers. I will cooperate with
all legally authorized agencies and
their representatives in the pursuit
of justice.
I know that I alone am responsible
for my own standard of
professional performance and will
take every reasonable opportunity
to enhance and improve my level of
knowledge and competence.
I will constantly strive to achieve
these objectives and ideals,
dedicating myself before God to my*

chosen profession... law enforcement.

Let's look at this code written half a century ago and see how it is still relevant in today's modern world. We see in the first paragraph service to the community and protection of constitutional rights to all, as well as protection of the innocent from the ones who would do harm to them. That is your charge as an officer and as a leader of officers right there, nothing more, nothing less. Your job as a leader is to lead the followers to be stewards of the community, to teach them how to best protect the weakest among us, and how to fight the most-evil among us. As a young officer it is your job to be steadfast and true to the command. Some politicians and prosecutors as well as chief executives would do well to be reminded of this.

The second paragraph deals with the personal aspect. How many officers and leaders have been found lacking in this area? From corruption to murder, agencies have had to deal with all kinds of crimes within their ranks. The perception is that cops are corrupt when stories like that break, but the truth is cops are people too. You have bad doctors, lawyers, chefs, nurses. Any profession has their bad actors, organizations should be training young followers that corruption of any level is unacceptable and that reporting such behavior is commendable.

In the third paragraph we are instructed to follow the law and not let personal feelings dictate our action and to maintain our pursuit of justice. We are told not to let personal feelings and friendship dictate our actions. We are to be stewards of the system.

The badge in the next part is the outward symbol of our inner personality. If we allow the badge to be tarnished it is because our inner self was destroyed long before. Losing sight of one's inner moral compass will lead to ruin for an officer. Leaders need to be mindful of that among their rank and file.

The final paragraphs deal with personal standards and shows how we can have the best leaders in the world, but if we are not forthright in our own personal standards, we will fall short every time.

All officers need to remember this code and review it often, this is foundation for building a solid career, and this is also a good discussion starter on the question from the first chapter, why? These values and ethics found within this code will still be around, I think, well into the 21st century.

Afterword

In this book we have tried to cover various facets of leadership methods and the lessons from those methods. It is my sincere hope that you can take some valuable information from the material presented. Like most books on leadership that are out there, reading and studying them will not reveal all the answers or show you the secret handshake on how to be a leader, that comes with time and experience along with trial and error.

Hopefully, this book will cut out the error and can be used as a reference for the professional, whether public sector or private sector, on how to adapt these principles to their organization.

It is a wide-open time in our society as far as new, modern practices of being a leader is concerned, techniques have changed several times from when I first started my career. Leadership will continue to be an everchanging dynamic,
but the essence of leadership will forever be the same. It is not enough to just be conscious of new ideas and new ways of leading different personalities, you have to put it into practice. Many leaders are out of touch with the followers they purport to lead, they put

distance between themselves and the line. That is not, in my opinion, the best way to build a team network within an organization, and after all that is what we as leaders really want, everyone working for the same goal.

Lastly, enjoy the opportunity to be a leader. It is a rare thing to head an entire organization and leave a lasting, hopefully positive, imprint on the future no matter how long it lasts. Every new leader wants to separate themselves from the ones that came before, but always be learning the why of the actions. When you can answer the why, you can fundamentally change an organization and, by extension, the followers within the organization.

About the Author

Ronnie Ashmore is a two-time chief of police who started his law enforcement career as a jailer working his way up through the ranks.

He is the author of several short stories, crime, and western novels. This is his first non-fiction book. When he is not working or writing and has some spare time, he enjoys playing golf, fishing, and traveling with his wife and kids.

You can contact him at ronnieashmore@mail.com